Whales, dolphins, and porpoises, despite their fishlike form and total commitment to living in the sea, are mammals. They breathe air, bear their young live, and have hair. To scientists they are members of the order Cetacea. Cetaceans are commonly classified into three types— whales, dolphins, and porpoises—although most American scientists recognize them as simply whales or porpoises.

Whales are the stuff of legends; they are huge, powerful, and mysterious. Some we see often, yet we know little about them. Others prowl the vastness of the sea, unseen except by a fortunate few.

MORE FOR THE ADVANCING PIANIST

Succeeding with the Masters®—Compiled, edited, and recorded by Helen Marlais

Succeeding with the Masters®
Baroque Era, Volume Two   (FF1439)
Classical Era, Volume Two   (FF1437)
Romantic Era, Volume Two   (FF1441)

A groundbreaking collection of intermediate through early advanced authentic repertoire by the master composers of the Baroque, Classical, and Romantic eras, and the Twentieth Century. This series places the music in both a historical as well as social perspective and provides valuable practice strategies and a complete performance CD.

Succeeding with the Masters®
Student Activity Book,
Classical Era, Volume Two   (FF1658)

This activity book is full of enjoyable activities that will help your students learn about the master composers' lives and music. Students can complete all the activities by using the music, CD, composer biographies, and glossary in the Volume Two Performance Book.

Succeeding with the Masters®
Teacher's Handbook,
Classical Era, Volume Two   (FF1659)

Provides all of the answers for the *Student Activity Book* as well as some additional ideas for group activities. A recommended listening list is included for further enjoyment of classical music.

The Festival Collection®
Book 6   (FF1590)
Book 7   (FF1591)

A companion series to *Succeeding with the Masters®* covering the early intermediate to early advanced repertoire levels. Contains repertoire from the Baroque, Classical, and Romantic eras, and Twentieth/Twenty-First Centuries. Contains interesting information about the pieces and composers along with a complete performance CD.

The FJH Contemporary Keyboard Editions—Series Editor Helen Marlais

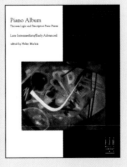

The FJH Contemporary Keyboard Editions is a series that focuses on the best contemporary music for keyboard of the late 20th and early 21st centuries. These collected works by some of today's leading art-music composers will expand a student's concept of rhythm, harmony, sound, and texture.

SOUND/ WORLD, A Collection of New Keyboard
Experiences, Volume 2, by Stan Applebaum   (J1010)

Modern Miniatures for Piano Solo,
Volume 2, by Dianne Goolkasian Rahbee   (J1011)

Piano Album, Thirteen Light and Descriptive
Piano Pieces, by Dimitar Ninov   (J1008)

Intuitive Journeys, by Wynn-Anne Rossi   (J1016)

Preludes, Volume 2,
by Dianne Goolkasian Rahbee   (J1018)

Watercolors for Ten Fingers,
by Martín Kutnowski   (J1021)

In Recital® with...
Edwin McLean
Kevin Olson

Edited by Helen Marlais

Railroad Blues
by C. Luckeyth Roberts / Haven Gillespie /
Howard Washington
arr. Edwin McLean

Perdido
by Ervin Drake / Harry Lenk / Juan Tizol
arr. Kevin Olson

Night Train
by Oscar Washington / Lewis Simpkins /
Jimmy Forrest
arr. Edwin McLean

This Masquerade
by Leon Russell
arr. Kevin Olson

Until This Moment
by Edwin McLean

Beale Street Blues
by W. C. Handy
arr. Edwin McLean

My Foolish Heart
by Victor Young / Ned Washington
arr. Kevin Olson

House of the Rising Sun
Traditional
arr. Edwin McLean

Off-Balance Blues
by Kevin Olson

The Saint Louis Blues
by W. C. Handy
arr. Kevin Olson

Unforgettable
by Irving Gordon
arr. Edwin McLean

In Recital® for the Advancing
Pianist—Jazz and Blues

• Musically-engaging jazz originals and
arrangements of jazz and blues gems
by Edwin McLean and Kevin Olson.

• Students play walking bass figures,
swing, bebop, boogie-woogie, traditional
blues, and stride bass; as well as jazz
ballads and Latin jazz.

• Beautiful jazz and blues repertoire for
year after year use.

FJH2087   US $7.50

6 74398 22593 4

ISBN-13: 978- 1-56939-795-4
ISBN-10: 1-56939-795-3

50750

9 781569 397954

THE FJH MUSIC COMPANY INC.
www.fjhmusic.com

Whales
Dolphins-Porpoises
OF THE PACIFIC

Many people are developing an affinity for whales as we learn more about these intelligent creatures. Yesterday's fearsome beast—or profitable resource—has become today's friend. These pilot whales, so-named for their habit of appearing to lead other whales, were once called blackfish.

Whales
Dolphins-Porpoises
OF THE PACIFIC
by Peter C. Howorth

Peter C. Howorth, who also wrote *Channel Islands: The Story Behind the Scenery*, is well known for his magazine articles and books about the sea. He collected whales and porpoises for oceanariums for several years, along with seals and sea lions. Today, Peter directs a nonprofit clinic for sick and injured marine mammals. He enjoys returning the animals to the sea with their health restored far more than he once enjoyed collecting them. Peter also participates in various scientific research projects involving marine mammals.

Front cover: Breaching humpback; photo by Dan McSweeney.
Pages 2 and 3: Gray whale feeding in kelp; photo by Howard Hall. This page: Sounding humpbacks; photo by Flip Nicklin.

Book Design by K. C. DenDooven, Edited by Mary Lu Moore

Third Printing, 1988
WHALES-DOLPHINS-PORPOISES OF THE PACIFIC. © 1985 KC PUBLICATIONS, INC.
LC 84-81847. ISBN 0-916122-98-0.

WHALE. The word conjures up images of immense size and power, of gentleness or savagery, and of familiarity somehow shrouded in mystery, for this largest of creatures remains a stranger to us in many ways. Our understanding of the whale is nearly as fragmentary and elusive as the mist of its spout.

We know a little more about the porpoise, if only because its comparatively small size and gentle demeanor make it easier to handle. But both animals live in the trackless immensity of the sea, where human observers can only seize fleeting glimpses into their life.

Unfortunately, our legacy is to know more of their death than of their life, for man has hunted many of these creatures to near extinction. The killing continues even today. Porpoises die in droves only because they follow tuna and salmon schools. Great whales still fall to the explosive harpoons of nations more interested in exploitation than in conservation.

What we have discovered of whales and porpoises is fascinating enough to open entirely new fields of inquiry. The study of whales is the ultimate challenge, for nowhere on land are the animals so huge and their environment so boundless.

Whales and porpoises have broken their ties with the land so effectively that their past

Some 40 tons of whale clear the surface as this humpback breaches off the Hawaiian coast. No one is certain why these leviathans leap out of the water. Are they showing off or making a threat? Such a sight is never forgotten, as whale-watching fans will readily attest.

is largely unknown to us. Even though they are mammals, they are so far removed from us on the evolutionary scale that merely describing them requires a different vocabulary. Common terrestrial terms often cannot do them justice.

The sea is their stronghold, because even a creature as large as a whale is hard to find there, especially if it wanders far from land in small groups. Even today, scientists feel that species unknown to man may roam the vast reaches of the sea.

For many, the only chance to see a whale is by going to an oceanarium. Marineland of the Pacific in Palos Verdes, California, was the oldest oceanarium on the west coast when it finally closed in 1987. We have learned a great deal about whales because of such institutions. Here, a trainer proves the killer whale can be gentle as it nimbly plucks a fish from his mouth.

7

The Largest Creatures on Earth

Before the mighty dinosaurs perished some 70 million years ago, a seemingly insignificant, insect-eating mammal had appeared. Soon, lacking competition from the giant reptiles, it prospered, using its peculiar attributes to singular advantage. Its warm blood and fur kept out the chill of the advancing ice age. This creature bore its young live and cared for them as they grew, insuring the continuance of its kind. And its relatively complex brain endowed it with acute senses and a blossoming intelligence unknown to its predecessors.

In time, this animal branched into two groups: the herbivores—plant-eaters—and the carnivores—flesh-eaters. These groups divided into many others, each to fill a particular ecological niche. Some, through selective adaptations, gradually returned to the sea. Such animals were probably evolutionary descendants of early *ungulates,* even-toed animals related to the cattle, sheep, and pigs of today.

The earliest known relatives of *cetaceans* (whales and porpoises) appeared more than 50 million years ago. These first *archaeocetes* ("ancient whales"), known as *Prozeuglodons,* were about the size of today's porpoises. They had well-developed teeth, probably for grasping small fish. Their nostrils, unlike those of terrestrial mammals, had gradually moved up along their head until they were midway between their snout and their cranium; thus they could breathe without lifting their head. Also, they could keep their eyes submerged for an uninterrupted view of their liquid environment.

Zeuglodons appeared some ten million years later, slender, 70-foot-long creatures so reptilian in appearance that scientists first thought they were marine dinosaurs and dubbed them *Basilosaurus,* a name largely discounted today. Like their predecessors, the Zeuglodons were probably fish-eaters, for they had rows of porpoiselike teeth and blowholes on top of their head.

Such creatures flourished in the western portion of the ancient Tethys Sea, which overlapped the present Mediterranean. Later, this sea likely opened up to the Indian Ocean near the present Suez Canal, to the Baltic via Europe, and to the Central Atlantic between Europe and Africa. An additional channel may have cut across Nigeria to the South Atlantic. Thus, the expanding sea allowed these primitive relatives of cetaceans to spread. Cetaceans would soon populate all the seas.

Like a Jules Verne creation, this huge humpback parts the waves.

THE FIRST TRUE WHALES

What happened next is buried in the Early Oligocene rocks of 35 million years ago, for Zeuglodon seems to have reached an evolutionary dead end, or else any direct link it may have had to modern cetaceans is missing.

The next creatures to appear were very similar to some of today's. Called *Squalodonts* because their teeth resembled those of sharks (*squalus* means shark), they probably were the ancestors of at least one family of contemporary porpoises.

More than 26 million years ago, early relatives of modern baleen whales appeared. No older fossils have been unearthed to link these whales to their ancestors, but scientists believe they descended from ancient toothed whales. The ancestors of today's toothed whales did not appear until shortly after the early baleen whales, and their links to earlier forms were also buried in the past.

Of today's whales, the gray is probably most closely related to the ancient baleen whales. Fossil remains of grays perhaps as much as 200,000 years old have been found near San Pedro, California. Gray whales lived in the North Atlantic until several hundred years ago, then disappeared.

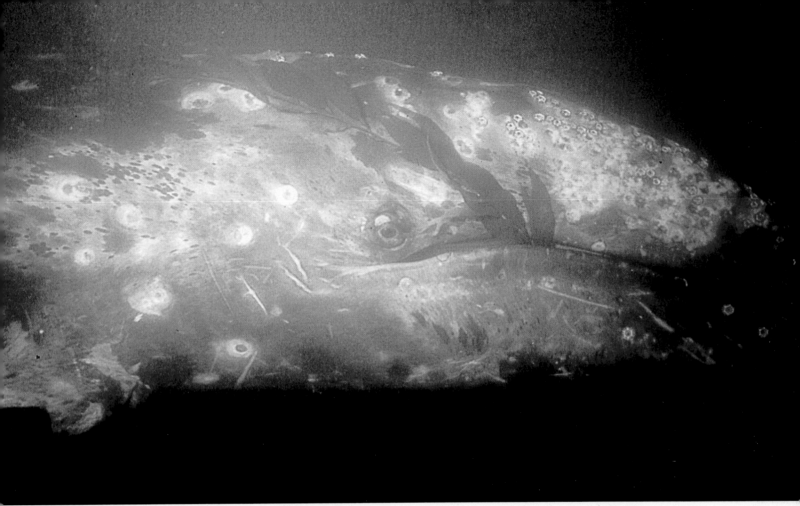

The familiar gray whale was swimming off our shores long before man arrived. The gray is a baleen whale. Instead of teeth, it has rows of brushlike baleen plates for straining tiny organisms from the sea. This gray whale is combing the kelp for isopods, buglike animals that superficially resemble earwigs.

Toothed whales far outnumber baleen whales. Despite the false killer whale's menacing name and formidable appearance, it is nothing more than a large dolphin. This particularly amiable specimen lives at Sea Life Park in Hawaii. Instead of straining shrimplike creatures from the water, this animal chases down fast-moving fish and squid.

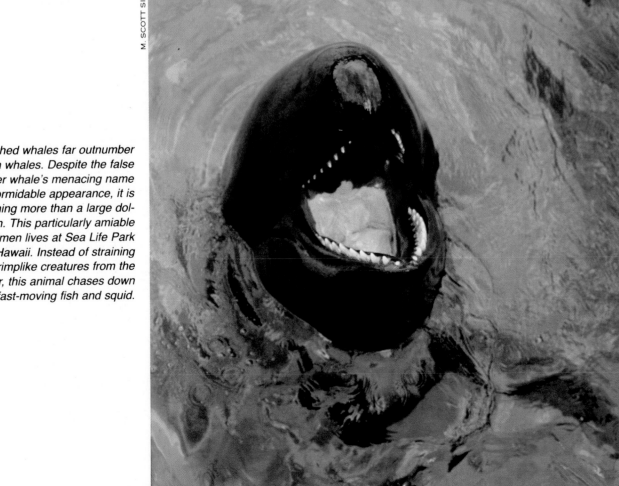

With so many missing fossil links, it seems surprising that even this comprehensive a cetacean history is known. Clues can be gleaned from other sources, however. For one thing, we know from embryological studies that developing cetaceans grow the hind limbs of terrestrial mammals, only to have them disappear as the fetus progresses. Even after they are born, cetaceans possess rudimentary pelvic bones. These are not without function, for even though they are buried in muscle tissue and are not connected to other bones, they do serve as an anchor for the male's reproductive organ.

Moreover, all cetaceans have teeth or tooth buds in the early stages of development. These disappear in the *mysticetes* ("moustache whales") to be replaced in function by baleen plates, brushlike structures for straining food from the water. Even cetacean blood provides clues to the past, for the composition of its serum protein resembles that of the ruminants, or cud-chewing animals. Also, cetacean stomachs are divided into three chambers.

Strangely enough, many cetaceans even behave like ruminants. They form groups called pods rather than herds. Some will even follow a leader to certain death. They can be curious or suspicious about anything new in their environment. Some use their head to butt other creatures. Males may even butt one another. Their mating is very brief, and the calves are able to move on their own shortly after they are born. Whether these traits are inherited or have developed out of necessity is unknown, but most of them do help these animals survive in a hostile environment.

As unfriendly as the sea may seem at times, it is the only place where animals as large as the great whales can survive. No bones are strong enough to support their weight on land; no limbs are powerful enough to move them. Indeed, no muscles are even tough enough to simply expand their chest for breathing—which is why whales die when they become stranded on beaches.

Elephants seem large, but a whale's tongue can weigh more. The dinosaurs were huge; yet the biggest ones actually lived semiaquatic lives, their massive bulk supported in part by water. Only the sea could have spawned the great whales; only the sea can support them.

PETER J. BRYANT

A Fishlike Mammal Emerges

Although Aristotle in his great wisdom recognized cetaceans as mammals, many subsequent observers did not. This was more a tribute to the extent that cetaceans had adapted to their environment than a lack of acumen on the observers' part, because they had scant opportunities for seeing the animals alive—as warm-blooded, air-breathing creatures.

Cetaceans are fishlike, although their tail flukes, or lobes, are horizontal rather than vertical. Halibut and other flatfish have similar tails, which are perfectly suited for rocketing upward from the sea floor to seize prey. In the case of cetaceans, the flukes allow the animals

Whales often travel together in pods. Their social habits help them to survive the savage sea. Safety in numbers, plus a greater ability to find food, is probably among the benefits of traveling together. These humpbacks are spouting in perfect unison.

Baleen consists of tough, resilient structures like teeth on a huge comb. Each tooth feathers into dense, brushlike filaments capable of straining tiny animals out of the sea.

GARY L. FRIEDRICHSEN

The common dolphin is a toothed cetacean. Its form is adapted for swiftness and agility. It has many vertebrae, allowing tremendous flexibility throughout its length. Its neck bones, however, are fused together so that its neck will remain rigid. This helps streamline its movements. Its forelimbs are modified into flippers, and the hind limbs have disappeared. The dolphin's brain is quite large. Much of it is geared toward interpreting sounds.

to swim to the surface to breathe, then return to the depths to feed. It seems strange that the flukes have no bones, but this is only a reflection of how well the cetaceans have adapted to their environment over the ages.

The flukes are driven by powerful muscles connected to the spine. Chevron-shaped bones on the underside of the last several vertebrae and spines on top provide additional surface area for the attachment of muscles. The spine itself has more vertebrae than the spine of most land mammals. Each vertebra is relatively short, allowing tremendous flexibility. The neck vertebrae are sometimes fused together, however, so that head movements will not break the streamlined form of the animal.

The skull is massive, sometimes dominating one third the length of the skeleton. Huge jaws account for most of the skull's length. The rib cage varies in cetaceans; whales generally have a comparatively small chest, while porpoises have a relatively large one. The rear ribs float; that is, they are not connected by a sternum. This allows for a tremendous expansion of their lungs as well as for the collapse of their lungs during deep dives.

The flippers, like our arms, are attached to the shoulder blade with a ball joint, but there the similarity ends, for the bones of the flipper form a rigid fin. The flippers are similar in function to the control surfaces on an airplane wing. They can be angled for diving or surfacing, or tilted independently for rolling or turning. Maximum speed is attained when they are flat against the body. When the flippers are fully extended, the animal slows down.

Some cetaceans have dorsal fins. Though not supported by bone, they are generally rather rigid and provide directional stability. Dorsals probably also make fast turns possible, acting much like a surfboard fin in preventing slippage.

The area forward of the tail also aids in turning, because it is usually flat and tall. This shape creates very little resistance, but provides quite a "bite" for turning. Like the dorsal fin, this ridge probably aids in directional stability, working like the keel of a boat. Its form also provides support for up-and-down tail movements and flexibility for turning.

The overall body shape of the cetacean is somewhere between a cigar and a teardrop. Designers of submarines have imitated this superior form to advantage.

Suggested Reading

Gaskin, D. F. *Ecology of Whales and Dolphins.* London, England: Heinemann, 1982.

Matthew, Harrison L. *The Natural History of the Whale.* New York: Columbia University Press, 1958.

Ridgway, Sam H. *Mammals of the Sea.* Springfield, Illinois: Charles G. Thomas, 1972.

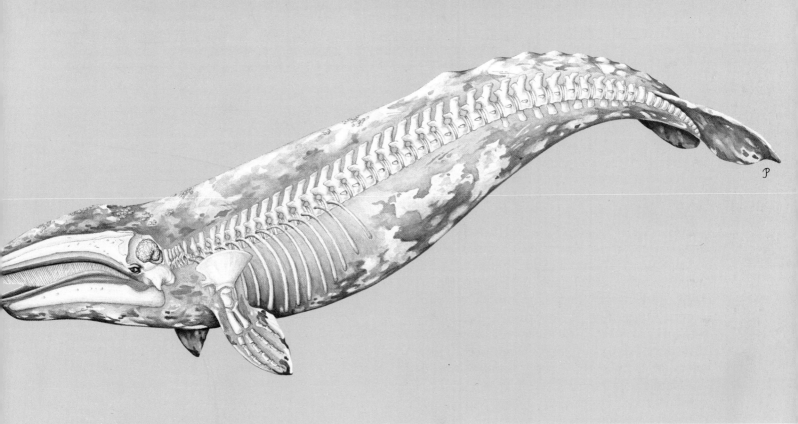

ILLUSTRATIONS BY JANN POPSON

The gray whale, like most baleen whales, has a smaller brain in relation to its body size than does the dolphin. Unlike toothed whales, baleen whales probably do not use sonar to locate prey, thus the part of their brain that would be used in interpreting sonar sounds is not well developed. Also, baleen whales have a comparatively small chest.

The towering dorsal fin of the killer whale may act like a keel, reducing slippage when the animal turns abruptly. Although the fin may measure more than five feet in height, it is supported entirely by cartilage. The prominent fin, the streamlined body, and the blunt, rounded nose are all features reflected in a far more ominous way by nuclear submarines.

CHIP MATHESON

Monarchs of the Sea

It has been said that some cetaceans use their muscles several times more efficiently than any other mammal. One scientist even concluded that porpoises theoretically could not have enough muscle power to swim as fast as they do. He based his conclusions on the power required to move a rigid shape, patterned after a porpoise, through the water.

But no cetacean is rigid; therein lies the pitfall of his intriguing theory. Flexibility actually increases speed. The porpoise's thin porous outer layer of skin absorbs minute vibrations caused by turbulence created by water resistance. Moreover, the blubber layer, which streamlines the body shape, ripples as the animal accelerates, causing wrinkles to remain in certain places under high speed. The ridges correspond to low-pressure areas; the dimples to high-pressure regions. Thus, swirls of turbulence cannot form around the porpoise's body and reduce its speed.

As efficient as they are, porpoises are not as fast as many think. They can cut in toward the side of a fast-moving boat, then ride its bow wave, thus giving the illusion that they can easily travel at more than 20 knots (nearly 23 miles an hour). Most porpoises actually reach only 14 to 16 knots. At least one species exceeds 20 knots, but only in short sprints.

Bow-riding is a remarkable phenomenon in itself. Judging its speed with precision, the porpoise can burst in on the beam of a fast vessel and take up station just under the bow. The porpoise will position its flukes so the water upwelling from the bow will push against them, thus driving the animal forward with scant effort on its part. The porpoise thus planes along ahead of the bow wave, comfortably supported by the rush of water under its pectoral fins.

Some whales swim even faster than porpoises. The sperm whale probably reaches 20 knots, while the killer whale likely exceeds that. The huge blue may reach 30, and the sei (pronounced "say") may be faster yet.

While the speed of some cetaceans is impressive, their diving ability is even more so. A sperm whale can descend to at least three quarters of a mile and hold its breath for an hour. The killer whale can reach a depth of 3,400 feet, while the pilot whale can dive to 2,000 feet. Even the bottlenose dolphin can swim downward at least 1,000 feet.

How can they do it?

ROBERT L. PITMAN

The sperm whale of Moby Dick *fame has a distinctive square snout. Some whales can be identified solely by their blow.*
The sperm whale spouts a "bushy" plume forward and to the left.

These common dolphins burst out of the water in an explosive sprint. One bizarre theory to explain the speed of dolphins maintains that they are constantly sloughing off an extremely thin layer of skin. In other words, resistance is lessened because the animals are continually leaving their skin behind. Not surprisingly, many researchers scoff at this concept.

study in speed, the slender rthern right whale dolphin ps just ahead of the bow of essel. This is the only st coast dolphin that lacks dorsal fin.

When a whale prepares to dive, it inhales. Because its nostrils are on top of its head, it wastes no effort lifting its head to breathe, nor does it break its easy swimming rhythm. Its lungs are high on its body, which may ease the muscular effort required to expand them against the water pressure. The more relaxed the animal is, the more energy it can conserve for the dive. The exchange of gases in the lungs is nearly complete with each breath, whereas in humans, only 10 to 15 percent of the air is renewed with each breath.

When the whale dives, its blowhole clamps shut, sealing out water. Its epiglottis, near the base of its tongue, fits into the nasal passage, sealing it off so the animal can feed underwater even as it holds its breath.

Whale blood is rich in hemoglobin, which holds oxygen and carries it to the muscles and organs. The muscles are laced with myoglobin, which retains oxygen in the tissues. As the whale submerges, its heart rate slows, reducing the flow of blood to all but the vital organs and even storing some in an elaborate network of vessels called the *retia mirabilia* ("wonderful net"). This blood can then seep to the vital organs as the minutes pass underwater.

Meanwhile, the muscles may function without oxygen from the blood, obtaining it instead from the myoglobin in the tissues. Carbohydrates can be oxidized to release energy, with lactic acid as a byproduct of the process. The animal is highly tolerant of lactic acid, the compound that produces muscle fatigue. When the whale takes in oxygen again on the surface, the lactic acid is broken down. Carbon dioxide from the whale's metabolic processes is also eliminated at this time.

As the whale descends, the air in its lungs is compressed. This does not involve a relatively large volume, however, because the whale's lungs are rather small in comparison to its overall size (one to three percent as contrasted to seven percent for man). As the water pressure increases, the lungs collapse completely and air is squeezed into the airways, where no further exchange of air into the bloodstream can take place.

Nearly 80 percent of air is nitrogen, which does not pass out of the tissues and bloodstream as quickly as other gases do. Because a human diver breathes compressed air from tanks *underwater,* he takes in huge volumes of *compressed* nitrogen. If he ascends too rapidly,

DIANA RYAN McINTYRE

A whale's nostrils are placed on top of its head so it can swim easily without breaking stride. This fin whale's blowholes are protected from spray by a ridge.

the nitrogen bubbles expand in his bloodstream, rupturing tissues, thus causing the "bends." But the whale takes in air on the surface, so the nitrogen bubbles in its bloodstream can expand only to their original size as the whale ascends. Thus the whale does not get the bends.

When the whale surfaces, the telltale spout shoots skyward in a plume of mist. Some scientists maintain that the warm breath of the whale simply condenses as it reaches the cooler atmosphere, but this does not explain spouts in hot regions. Other researchers claim that the forceful exhalation vaporizes water pooled up outside the blowhole, or that some water is taken into the lungs under pressure. A few authorities say that when air squeezes past the nostrils, it is compressed and heats up. Once in the atmosphere, the pressure and heat would be reduced, causing the air to expand and cool, condensing into the familiar spout.

Most whales breathe a few times after they surface, then dive again. Deep-diving animals like the sperm whale may take up to 60 breaths before returning to the depths. Old whalers called this "having his spoutings out."

Humpback whales are noted for their spectacular breaching activities. Many humpbacks congregate off the Hawaiian Islands in winter, leaping almost completely out of the water, then falling back with a resounding splash. Humpbacks also frequent Glacier Bay, Alaska, where they repeat such antics in summer. As humpbacks breach, they sometimes twist and land on their backs, their flippers held in haphazard positions. Here, an enormous flipper shows amid the spray.

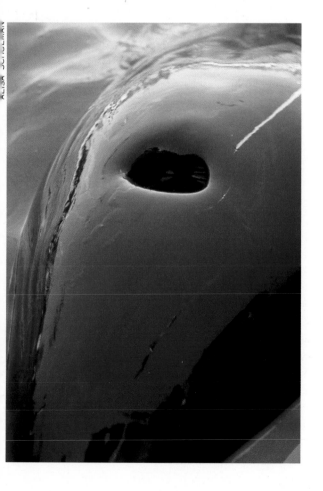

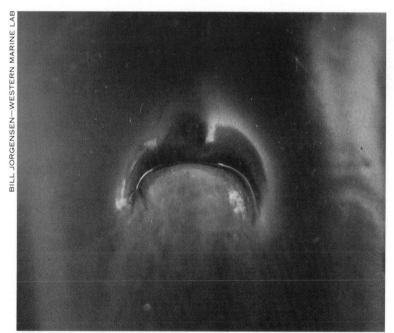

Smaller toothed cetaceans, like the killer whale on the left, have a single blowhole. The moment the animal surfaces, the blowhole opens and the animal expels its breath. The animal then inhales and the blowhole clamps shut. The whole process can be completed in a split second, especially if the animal is moving rapidly. Underwater, the blowhole is clamped tightly shut by a muscular, crescent-shaped flap. The closed blowhole of a Pacific white-sided dolphin is shown above.

When the porpoise dives, a similar process takes place. The porpoise's lungs are quite a bit larger in relation to its body. Thus, the animal can take in more oxygen, which probably enables it to chase down prey more efficiently because the power of its muscles is determined by how much oxygen they receive. Interestingly, the Dall porpoise, a very fast animal, holds three times more oxygen in its blood than does the slower bottlenosed dolphin. Moreover, the Dall has twice as much blood.

Authorities once believed that whales lacked a well-developed sense of touch. This friendly gray whale being rubbed and scratched could leave if it wished, but evidently it enjoys the attention.

These Dall porpoises with their striking black-and-white markings resemble miniature killer whales. They are extremely swift, powerful swimmers.

BEYOND THE FIVE SENSES

The sense of touch may also be linked to a cetacean's speed. A porpoise's skin hosts many cells sensitive to touch. These may automatically signal when the blubber should be wrinkled so that the animal's progress through the water will be streamlined with no conscious effort on its part. Also, nerve endings at the base of whiskers may serve as speedometers in many cetaceans, the vibrating hairs telegraphing the speed to the brain. (All cetaceans have whiskers; if not as adults, then at least during fetal development.) Cetaceans in general seem to be sensitive to touch, particularly during lovemaking—but they probably also enjoy a gentle rub or scratch.

Perhaps because the blubber layer beneath the skin is relatively insensitive to pain and cold, scientists once felt that touch was not an important sense to cetaceans. But the portion of the brain concerned with touch is significant and should not be discounted, particularly since cetaceans may not always use this sense in the same ways we do.

This is not true for smell, because cetaceans seem to have little need for it. The organs of smell have all but disappeared, and even the section of brain normally used for this sense is essentially undeveloped. But linked to smell is taste, and cetaceans probably do utilize this sense to some extent, if only to sample the water.

Cetaceans see well, but only for short distances, because even in the clearest water, visibility is not much better than it is during a thick fog on land. Moreover, the deeper the

water becomes, the more the sunlight is filtered out. Even in extremely clear water, darkness is eternal beyond 1,500 feet or so.

To compensate for the darkness, cetaceans have *tapetums* in their eyes, mirrorlike plates that flip up as the light grows dimmer, bouncing lost light back into the retina. The eyes themselves are shaped so the animals can see well underwater, but not above—the exact opposite of land mammals. The cornea is protected by a tough membrane. As might be expected, tear ducts are lacking; instead, a thin, oily substance lubricates the eyes.

Many creatures, especially large whales, cannot see straight ahead. Porpoises and some small toothed whales can, perhaps making it easier to chase down prey as they close in for the kill. But how do cetaceans initially locate their prey in a world of perpetual fog?

Sound travels several times faster underwater than it does on land. We can seldom hear creatures underwater because our ears are not adapted to the environment, but the silent world is anything but serene. Shrimp make noises, especially when they travel in large shoals. Fish are audible as they swim; some even call to one another. And when any creature breaks the surface, its presence is broadcast everywhere.

Cetaceans have evolved a unique way of hearing underwater. No external lobes funnel sounds to the eardrums; the lobes have been sacrificed for streamlining. The openings that lead to the eardrums are all but closed. Even on a large whale the orifices are no larger than a wooden match, and they are still more constricted farther in. Because of these anatomical features, scientists once felt that cetaceans were essentially deaf.

Actually, cetaceans hear rather well. The ear canals are blocked because water is almost the same density as the tissues of the animals; a water-filled canal would prevent them from discerning the direction of the sounds. (This is why we cannot interpret sound direction accurately underwater.) Bones conduct sound vibrations too, further confusing the signal. To compensate for these problems, the inner ear of cetaceans is filled with an oily foam which insulates each hearing mechanism from vibrations from the surrounding bones and tissues. The animals can easily distinguish the direction a sound is coming from because each hearing mechanism is acoustically isolated from the other.

PETER J. BRYANT

Even the eye of a gray whale calf seems old and wise. The eye, larger than a baseball, is shaped so the animal can focus on objects beneath the sea. Out of the water, the whale probably sees less than we do underwater without a face mask.

When a cetacean dives, the water pressure against the ears is equalized by more oily bubbles squeezed in from surrounding cavities. Because the oil suspending the bubbles is virtually incompressible, the bubbles persist even under tremendous pressure, continuing to deflect unwanted vibrations from the hearing mechanism.

When baleen whales call to one another, they often use a very loud but low-frequency sound that can be discerned over considerable distances. Many toothed whales and porpoises emit sounds of a much higher frequency, however. These "clicks" are used to locate prey as well as to examine their surroundings. (The bat, another mammal that cannot use vision to locate its prey, also utilizes *echolocation*. Its hearing is even more acute.)

The clicking sounds are probably made in the nasal passage, since vocal cords are lacking. These clicks are focused in a tight beam. At least one scientist feels that the skull shape of certain cetaceans may act as a parabolic reflector of sound waves, which are then focused into a beam by the oil-filled, bulbous forehead, or melon, as it is called. The shape of the melon supposedly can be consciously altered by the animal, thus adjusting the focus.

CHRIS NEWBERT

Blainville's whale, sometimes called the dense-beaked whale, is seldom seen. It probably spends much of its time far offshore. A few have been seen off Hawaii, but only one has been reported for the west coast.

CHRIS NEWBERT

The pygmy killer whale reaches about eight feet in length. It is not common, although it turns up occasionally off Hawaii. These whales often swim abreast of one another.

BILL JORGENSEN—WESTERN MARINE LAB

This stranded minke, sometimes called the little piked whale, is the smallest of the west coast baleen whales. It feeds on small fish, squid, and krill.

Certainly the sound beams must be focused somehow, otherwise the echoes would be scattered and confused.

Porpoises and perhaps some whales probably home in on objects by moving their head from side to side, much as we turn toward a sound to determine the direction it came from. Sound reception in such animals is very keen, because the lower jaw, filled with an oil that conducts sound six times better than water, butts up against the inner ear. As the animal gets closer to an object, it emits a faster series of sounds that can determine the position, speed, size, shape, texture, and even the composition of the object.

Interestingly, experiments indicate that porpoises at least do not seem to be able to visualize what they have located by sound. They will persist in bouncing sound pulses off an object even when they can see it clearly. Perhaps their vision is used simply to zero in on an object at close range, because their sound beams probably convey more information.

THE LARGEST BRAIN

The great variety of sounds produced by cetaceans, as well as their rather large brain, has led some researchers to believe we may be able to communicate with them. The cetacean brain is indeed larger than ours, but size does not necessarily imply intelligence, especially as we perceive it. Actually, the size of their brain in proportion to their body is smaller than ours. Their brain is complex, indicating they are capable of processing a great deal of information, but much of it is developed toward hearing, especially in the toothed cetaceans.

The success of any creature depends upon how well it has adapted for survival in its environment. Whales are monarchs of the sea, for no other type of animal is known to prey consistently upon them. Their acute senses are used mainly for finding food and examining their surroundings. Most have little to fear from predators. True, the killer whale is an enemy, but only to a few other cetaceans. Man is the true enemy, for his technology has advanced so rapidly that no species can possibly evolve the intelligence necessary to elude him.

Before we try to assess a cetacean's intelligence from our viewpoint, we should pause and recognize its supremacy of the sea. We should remember what its brain is actually

The Pacific white-sided dolphin is a curious, friendly creature that often will accompany boats. Sometimes it rides just ahead of the bow; at other times it cavorts in the wake or makes aerobatic leaps to either side of the vessel.

Risso's dolphins resemble pilot whales in form, but they are much lighter in color, ranging from pale gray to white. Oddly, they are born light gray, then turn brown or nearly black as they grow. As they mature, their skin turns light again. The numerous dark scratches may be caused by scuffles with other dolphins or possibly by nips from squid beaks. Risso's dolphins prey heavily upon squid, swimming right into the schools.

Pacific spotted dolphins are divided into three separate populations. The coastal group ranges from Baja California south; the offshore pods travel along either side of the equator to within sight of the Mexican coast; and the Hawaiian population favors the waters off the islands. Animals from each group are marked differently from the other populations. These Hawaiian specimens have few spots, while individuals from the coast are extensively spotted.

The striped dolphin is readily distinguished from other species by the white streak pointing toward the dorsal fin. It also sports a dark band stretching from its eye to behind its belly.

STEVE SWARTZ

ROBERT L. PITMAN

Bottlenosed dolphins are highly vocal, chattering away with squeaks, clicks, and whistles. Some sounds are used for detecting prey. Others are used perhaps for signaling each animal's position and identity to others in a group. Unlike many other species, the bottlenosed dolphin has a flexible neck that enables it to turn its head for a quick look.

Overleaf: The mighty flukes of a diving humpback attest to its tremendous strength. Photo by Deborah Glockner-Ferrari

GARY L. FRIEDRICHSEN

used for and attempt to interpret the information it processes. To try to speak to an intelligence geared chiefly toward utilizing a sense we do not even possess is like someone who has always been blind trying to tell us what sight is like. In fact, it is even more difficult, for not only are we unable to naturally produce the same vocal sounds, we can't even speak the language—if it can be called that.

Many animals are capable of vocalizing emotions. A dog yelping in pain, a porpoise squeaking in distress, a man screaming in terror: all express genuine emotions; none is speaking a language. A wolf can call to others in its pack, signaling its position and even its identity. So can a whale, but this is not a language either. A parrot can imitate a person's voice, but the parrot is far from being an intellectual giant.

True language is a demonstration of intelligence as we know it. When vocalizations can express past, present, and future, and when they can be phrased into new combinations to express rational thoughts, then they form a language. As far as we know, cetaceans do not do this.

Man's intelligence has developed through communication in the form of language. This has been essential to our very existence, because we are quite helpless until we learn to survive in our environment. Cetaceans, even at birth, have little need for language. They can swim almost immediately; they are protected and fed by others; and they can learn how to survive merely by example. This does not imply that they lack intelligence, but rather that it is foolish to measure their intelligence by our standards.

STEVE LEATHERWOOD

This unusual creature is a cross between a rough-toothed dolphin and a bottlenosed dolphin. Having one in an oceanarium like Sea Life Park in Hawaii provides an opportunity for viewing as well as for studying it.

Suggested Reading

BURTON, ROBERT. *The Life and Death of Whales.* New York: Universe Books, 1973.

COFFY, D. J. *Dolphins, Whales and Porpoises.* New York: Collier Division of MacMillan Publishing Company, 1977.

ELLIS, RICHARD. *The Book of Whales.* New York: Alfred Knopf, 1980.

NORRIS, KENNETH. *The Porpoise Watcher.* New York: W. W. Norton and Company, 1974.

With enviable grace, speed, and power, a spinner dolphin breaks the barrier between air and water. This animal is named for its habit of spinning as it leaps.

The rough-toothed dolphin has a pointed snout that tapers gently into the head region, giving it something of a sharklike profile.

Pacific white-sided dolphins are capable of spectacular leaps, which made them a popular attraction at Marineland of the Pacific in Palos Verdes, California. People who work with them often call them lags, shortened slang for their scientific generic name, Lagenorthnchus, meaning "flask beak." Pacific white-sided dolphins do have a short, stubby beak, but it is difficult to see when the animals are moving swiftly.

The Gentlest Carnivores

All cetaceans, gentle as they usually are, are carnivores. The great baleen whales feed by straining creatures from the water through their brushlike baleen plates, while toothed whales and porpoises snap up their prey.

Largely because of their dentition, cetaceans are divided into two scientific orders: the baleen whales, or *mysticetes*, and the toothed cetaceans, or *odontocetes*. Each order is broken down into several families. The breakdown is reasonably clear-cut from a scientific standpoint.

When common names are used, this tidy breakdown disintegrates. Some cetaceans are popularly called dolphins; others, porpoises. Authorities have contrived neat definitions to overcome this confusion, but exceptions to their rules only cloud the issue. A few dolphins are called whales, and certain whales are called dolphins. The most ambiguous name of all is the northern right whale dolphin.

A porpoise is a small, toothed cetacean. It's as simple as that. Some porpoises are called just that; others are popularly named dolphins —but they are all porpoises, at least to most American scientists. Whales are cetaceans that have either teeth or baleen plates and usually exceed 14 feet in length. Three cetaceans are smaller than this but are still called whales because they resemble larger species (pygmy sperm whales, dwarf sperm whales, and pygmy killer whales). The melon-headed whales, which grow to only seven and a half feet, would seem to be an exception, but they closely resemble pygmy killer whales.

The Biters

Toothed cetaceans far outnumber baleen whales. The largest is no stranger to anyone who has read *Moby Dick.* Yet in many ways the sperm whale remains a mystery to us.

No one is certain why this animal·has a huge, oil-filled forehead, but this has not stopped researchers from coming up with several fascinating explanations. One scientist maintains that the oil is used to absorb carbon dioxide. Another feels that the reservoir is used as a buoyancy tank. When the supply of warm blood to the cavity is cut down as the whale dives and cold water shoots down the left nasal passage—which runs through the cavity—the oil condenses, hardening into a wax that is not as buoyant as the fluid. When the blood returns, the oil supposedly expands into a buoyant liquid again.

HEINZ SCHATZ

This perpetually smiling Cuvier's beaked whale is rarely seen by most people. It probably spends much of its life well offshore, diving deeply for its prey. It has only two teeth, both on the tip of the lower jaw.

ROBERT L. PITMAN

This rare view of two northern right whale dolphins shows their distinctive markings and shape. They are extremely slender and streamlined animals capable of swimming very swiftly.

...e pilot whale was dubbed ...othead" by whaling crews, ... uncomplimentary but ...hly descriptive nickname. ... bulbous black forehead ...tinguishes it from other ...all whales. The pilot whale ...ds extensively on squid, ...t will eat other things, too.

ROBERT PITMAN—EARTHVIEWS

The white "moustache" and chin, coupled with the rounded tips of the flippers, identify this animal as a pygmy killer whale. This cetacean inhabits tropical waters of the Pacific.

The sperm whale's blowhole is set off to its left side. Inside the sperm whale's head is spermacetti, *an oil prized by whalers.*

Another theory suggests that the oil-filled chamber conducts sounds produced in one of the nasal passages. These sounds are then reflected off the curved shape of the front of the skull—colorfully dubbed Neptune's Chariot by Yankee whalers—and beamed forward.

The sperm whale probably does echolocate its prey, for it sometimes hunts in abysmal blackness, grappling with giant squid thousands of feet down. It eats small squid as well.

Sperm whales, along with porpoises and other toothed whales, may even stun their prey by beaming tremendous volumes of sound at them. Several times, fish have been observed swimming erratically, in a confused manner, just before they were gobbled up by echolocating cetaceans. Even though cetaceans sometimes do produce an incredible magnitude of sound, other scientists feel that cetaceans may simply chase their prey until it tires, then gulp it down.

Killer whales are something of a paradox. In captivity they are often surprisingly gentle and cooperative. But in the wild they are supreme predators, capable of devouring seals, sea lions, walruses, and porpoises. They even prey on the great whales. Their awesome abilities have earned them a formidable reputation. Like most top-level predators, however, killers cull out the weakest and slowest of large prey. Probably they actually rely upon fish and squid for the bulk of their diet, feeding on marine mammals only when the opportunity arises.

Killer whales track their prey by a variety of methods. Their hearing is acute, while their echolocating abilities are finely tuned. Like other odontocetes, they may stun their prey with sound. Finally, unlike all other cetaceans, killers poke their head out of the water to look for prey, spotting seals sprawled on ice cakes and rocks.

Killer whales hunt in packs like wolves when a larger quarry appears. They apparently wear down or cripple their prey by clamping onto its flippers or tail. They push their quarry hard, trying to prevent it from surfacing to breathe so it will soon become exhausted. Despite such coordinated attacks, large whales often escape. Fearsome scars remain as evidence of such encounters.

Although porpoises—even wild ones—are renowned for their friendly demeanor, they are also quite ruthless and efficient predators. Small schooling fish and squid make up the preferred diet of most porpoises, although a few eat shrimplike crustaceans as well. Like other toothed cetaceans, porpoises echolocate their prey and perhaps even immobilize it with sound beams.

30

GREGORY HAMMANN

The sperm whale's tail was something to be respected, even feared, for it could smash a whaleboat into matchwood with a single blow.

Oregon residents were electrified when a pod of huge sperm whales beached themselves near Florence. No one has been able to explain this suicidal behavior, although several other species of cetaceans are also known to deliberately strand themselves in large numbers.

The Gulpers and Skimmers

Although small schooling fish are an important part of the diet of many whales, *krill,* consisting of shrimplike creatures smaller than your little finger, is the staff of life for some species. Krill abounds in polar waters. Sometimes it is so thick the sea turns red.

Swimming through this living stew are the great whales. The rorquals, including blue, fin, sei, Bryde's (pronounced "BREW-ders") and minke whales, eat by gulping a mouthful of water, then forcefully expelling it with their huge tongue. Humpbacks feed in the same manner. This volume of water is augmented when the pleatlike longitudinal grooves under the chin and along the throat are expanded, much like the bellows of a concertina. This enables a large blue whale to take in up to 70 tons of water at a gulp.

As the water is forcefully expelled by the tongue, perhaps assisted by the throat muscles, the krill is strained out in the baleen plates, then swallowed. Baleen, like our fingernails and hair, is made from keratin. Baleen plates do not replace the teeth that disappear during fetal development; instead, they seem to emerge as extensions of the transverse ridges of the palate. The rorquals and humpbacks have short baleen plates that completely encircle the mouth, making efficient food strainers.

Some rorquals feed on their side near the surface, perhaps so they can turn quickly to encircle fast prey like fish. The fin whale feeds on its right side, which is white around the mouth; its other side is dark. White is more difficult to see from below, whereas black is harder to spot from above. This uneven coloring could serve two purposes: the bold markings could frighten fish toward the whale's mouth, and the color patterns could make it difficult to see the mouth itself.

Some whales slap their fins on the surface as they circle their prey, perhaps to herd them into a tight ball. The humpback blows a ring of bubbles around a school of fish, causing the fish to mill about in a confused circle, then surfaces in their midst, engulfing thousands in its cavernous mouth.

Gulping is a very efficient means of feeding. A blue whale can devour up to four tons of krill a day, or eight million tiny animals. The fin whale eats up to three tons, but the sei manages only a ton and a half.

Humpback whales are gulpers. They ingest huge volumes of water into their mouth, then strain out the food with their baleen as they push the water out with their tongue. Pleats along the throat expand with each gulp, allowing literally tons of water to be gulped. Note the distended throat of the whale on the right.

Bryde's whale is readily identified by three ridges that extend forward of the blowhole to the snout. No other baleen whale has these characteristics.

The blue whale, also a baleen whale, has a single ridge forward of the blow-hole and a broad, flat snout. It is the largest creature ever to evolve.

Two humpbacks perform a graceful underwater ballet off Hawaii. These huge creatures sing weird, haunting songs once popularized by a record album. No one is certain why they sing, although evidence suggests that only the males are involved. Possibly their singing is part of a courtship ritual or a means of asserting themselves among other males.

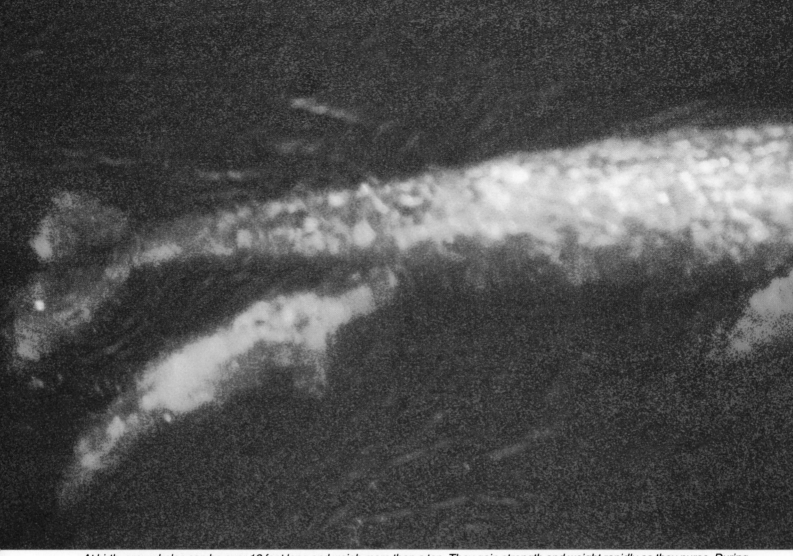

At birth, gray whales can be over 12 feet long and weigh more than a ton. They gain strength and weight rapidly as they nurse. During the first several months the calf stays very close to its mother, who protects as well as nurtures it. A gray whale mother can become extremely aggressive when its calf is threatened. Whalers called the gray "devilfish" with good reason.

An interesting ménage à trois often develops when gray whales breed. The large female in the middle is helped by another male on the right while her aroused suitor swims close by.

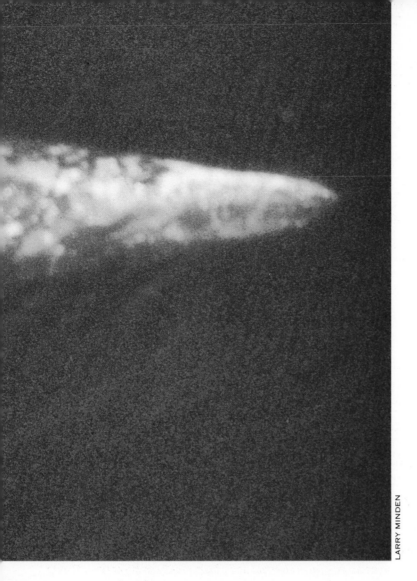

Sei whales obtain their food by skimming the surface with their mouth open as well as by gulping. But right whales are the true specialists in the art of skimming. Their baleen plates are quite long—up to 14 feet as compared to 3 or 4 feet for the rorquals. Moreover, the baleen of the right whale does not completely encircle the mouth. Instead, a gap in front allows water to rush into the mouth as the whale slowly swims along. Right whales lack pleated throat grooves, but since they feed by skimming, they don't really need them. Every so often the whale closes its mouth and swallows the krill trapped in the fine strands of baleen.

Although gray whales also feed by skimming, they are primarily bottom feeders. Grays usually plow a furrow along the sand or mud of the sea floor, straining out organisms that live there. They feed on their right side, which is often scraped nearly clean of barnacles around the mouth. The baleen on this side is shortened because it is used more.

Baleen whales, especially humpbacks, emit an intriguing variety of sounds. No evidence yet discovered proves they can echolocate.

THE LONGEST SWIM

Every year the gray whale migrates 6,000 or 7,000 miles down the coast, from the Bering Sea to Baja California, then returns. This is the longest migration of any mammal. How does the gray whale navigate over such a vast distance if it does not use echolocation? No one really knows, although several explanations are possible.

Some observers believe that the gray whale may find its way by rearing its head out of the water to spot landmarks. But most whales are notoriously nearsighted, especially out of the water. Besides, how could they obtain bearings on foggy days? Perhaps they simply follow the contours of the coast and of the sea floor, keeping the rising sun on their left on their way down, spurred by the vanguard of animals ahead of them. Possibly they learn the route by following others, later passing on their knowledge to new generations.

At any rate, in late fall the pregnant females head south, followed by the other females, and finally by the males. They travel in loosely knit groups of up to 16 animals, often cutting corners rather than hugging the coast. They eat little or nothing on the way.

Winter finds the grays congregated in the warm, protected lagoons of Baja California. As each calf is born, it is often helped to the surface by its mother, for its flippers usually emerge curled up from nearly 13 months of confinement in the womb. The calf swims quite well within just a few hours of its birth, however.

A newborn calf is about a third the length of its mother—more than 12 feet—and weighs over a ton. It doesn't have a rich blubber layer at birth, so warm water is essential for the nursery ground.

The calf gains weight very quickly because whale milk has ten times the fat content of cow milk. It nurses by nuzzling its mother's recessed nipples until she squirts a jet of milk into its mouth. The calf stays very close to its mother, who jealously protects it from all comers, killer whales and sharks included. The calf nurses at least seven months, if not closer to a year.

Mature females breed every other year because they will not accept a male's advances when they are nursing. Since half the overall population is male, each barren female is usually accompanied by two bulls. Rather than vie with another male for the female's favor, however, one bull may sometimes support the

mating pair, for it is difficult for such leviathans to couple in the water.

By March the gray whales leave the lagoons, heading north to their summer feeding
grounds. They stay quite close to shore on the
way back, often venturing into kelp beds,
sometimes to strain out the bugs that live
on the leaves. Otherwise they eat little, living
mostly on stored fat. Gray whales can lose up
to nearly 30 percent of their overall weight
during migration.

The young calves are vulnerable to killer
whales' attacks during their journey north-
ward. This may explain why grays frequent
the kelp beds. They would be harder to see
there. They would also be harder to echolocate,
because the gas-filled bulbs on kelp leaves re-
flect sonar signals.

Some grays, especially young ones, do not
go all the way to the Bering Sea. Instead, they
summer at several food-rich areas along the
coast from California to British Columbia. These
younger animals may linger in southern waters
because the freezing polar seas may simply be
too cold for them—at least until they can build
up a thick layer of blubber. The young animals expose far more of their surface area in
relation to their overall body size than larger
whales do, and water dissipates heat 25 times
faster than air. Paradoxically, whales need a
great deal of food to stay warm, yet the largest
concentrations of food are found in the icy
waters of the north.

Other baleen whales migrate, but not as
far, nor over such defined routes. Then too,
they do not calve and breed in shallow lagoons,
although nearly all of them do frequent polar
seas during the summer months. Most whales
seem to feed day and night while in the polar
grounds, heading south only when threatened
by the advance of the ice.

Bowhead whales are the least migratory of
all baleen whales and inhabit polar seas year
round. They can even break through thin ice
or lift it up to breathe. Conversely, Bryde's
whales stay in warmer water throughout the
year, thriving on fish and plankton.

Sperm whales tend to drift away from the
tropics during the summer, some bulls reach-
ing as far as the polar regions, but they have
no distinct migrational paths. Killer whales are
the most widely distributed of all cetaceans,
ranging from the ice floes of both poles to
the equator. Individual populations, however,
seem to remain in their own territories.

The pelagic red crab, a shrimplike creature, roams the sea
from Central America to California. Sometimes it is so
abundant that the sea turns red. Cetaceans are known to eat
this animal as well as krill—other shrimplike organisms found
in polar regions. Such creatures must be abundant, for large
whales can eat literally tons of them every day.

Other toothed whales and porpoises seem
to follow their prey throughout the year. Because water temperatures fluctuate from year
to year, the distribution of these cetaceans is
sporadic on the edges of their ranges, but it is
fairly predictable in their familiar haunts.

Suggested Reading

DAUGHERTY, ANITA E. Marine Mammals of California.
Sacramento, California: Department of Fish and
Game, 1972.

LEATHERWOOD, STEPHEN, and RANDALL R. REEVES.
The Sierra Club Handbook of Whales. San Fran-
cisco: The Sierra Club, 1983.

———, et al. Whales, Dolphins, and Porpoises of the
Eastern North Pacific and Adjacent Arctic Waters.
NOAA Technical Report NMFS Circular 444.
Seattle, Washington: U.S. Dept. of Commerce,
National Oceanic and Atmospheric Admin.,
National Marine Fisheries Service, 1982.

RICE, DALE W., and ALLEN A. WOLMAN. Life History
and Ecology of the Gray Whale. Stillwater, Okla-
homa: American Society of Mammalogists, 1971.

WATSON, LYLE. The Sea Guide to Whales of the World.
New York: E. P. Dutton, 1981.

The flukes of each whale have distinctive shapes, color patterns, and scars that make it possible to identify individuals from photos.

The baleen of this baby gray whale shows clearly as the calf hitches a ride on its mother's back. Gray whales bear their young in the lagoons of Baja California.

Gray whales sometimes stop for a snack in kelp beds, especially on their migration north. They mouth the kelp, then flush the buglike creatures living in the fronds into their baleen plates.

Man and Cetaceans

Almost always, every natural resource necessary for man's survival can be found in a given area. It takes perseverance, ingenuity, and a high degree of adaptability to ferret out such resources and thrive upon them, especially in hostile climes.

In the frozen lands of the north, a man must metabolize large quantities of fat to stay warm. This requires a substantial intake of rich meat. If man is to build anything on the treeless tundra, he must have materials. And finally, he must have light to brighten the insane darkness of the polar winters. The whale can provide all this—and more.

It is not surprising that the Eskimo people have relied upon whales as an important part of their subsistence for more than 3,500 years. The whale provided them with bones for framing huts, sleds, and boats when wood was not available. The baleen was bent into different shapes for a variety of purposes or was shredded into thongs for lashings. The gut was dried and cut into thongs, too.

Sometimes the entrails were pickled for food stores; they prevented scurvy. The meat and blubber were shared by the inhabitants of each village. Preserving food for the long winters was seldom a problem; the inhospitable environment of ice and snow actually helped those who strove to live there. The Eskimo hunters rendered much of the blubber into oil rather than freezing it. The oil was kept in seal skins and used for lamp fuel or for trading with inland tribes.

Today the Eskimo are still allowed to hunt cetaceans, taking only what is necessary for their own subsistence. But many use modern implements including bomb lances, snowmobiles, and outboard motors. This has generated a controversy between native whalers and conservationists, who maintain that the hunt is no longer a traditional one.

The bowhead whale is the most endangered of all species. Only a few thousand survive, even though the Eskimo feel that plenty of them still exist. Until an accurate bowhead census has been taken, it will be difficult to further restrict Eskimo whaling activities. Certainly they should be allowed to follow their old ways, but not at the expense of jeopardizing the very existence of the bowhead.

Other North American natives also hunted whales, although they do not today. The Aleut harpooned whales with spears dipped in aconite, a deadly poison. The lances were notched

PETER C. HOWORTH

GREG SILBER

Bowhead whales spend their entire life in Arctic regions. They can clear channels in thin ice and can even lift up ice to breathe. Because they must use channels through heavy ice, they become the prey of the Eskimo.

Eskimo whalers set out in an umiak *for their prey. Harpoons, ready for instant use, are stacked in the bow.*

othed cetaceans like this
lot whale are surprisingly
entle when captured, even
ough they could do their
ptors considerable harm.
his specimen is being
axed into a special structure
that it can be transported
an oceanarium.

WILLIAM M. MARQUETTE—NATIONAL MARINE MAMMAL LAB

The size of a whale is difficult to imagine. The blue whale is larger than any dinosaur. It can eat four tons of food in a day, but like most baleen whales, it is a rather gentle creature. It is most like a grazing animal in some ways, although it can be formidable when aroused. Compared to the whale, the dolphins seem tiny, yet man is even smaller.

so they would break off and work their way into the whale's vitals as it struggled. Indians of the Pacific Northwest were particularly accomplished whalers, pursuing their prey in long dugout canoes.

These natives of North America took only what they needed to survive. They probably helped the overall whale population by culling out weak, slow, and less intelligent individuals.

The Whalers

Tragically, the white man was the one who slaughtered whales in droves—not to feed struggling villagers, but to fill the coffers of a greedy few. As technology improved, even the fastest and most intelligent whales were unable to escape. Most were hunted until it was no longer economically feasible to pursue them. In many cases this meant they were perilously close to extinction.

In the 1880s the whaling industry provided products similar to those supplied by the petroleum industry of today. Whale blubber yielded oil for lighting and lubrication. Baleen, or whalebone as it was called, was widely used as a tough, flexible material replaced today by plastics. Flesh and bone were used as fertilizer or animal food. Teeth were carved into trinkets.

In the Old Country, whalers had chased their quarry just offshore in long, fast rowing craft, throwing a harpoon into them at point-blank range. Although this was not much more efficient than the Native American techniques, more whales were killed because they were sought for profit rather than for survival. All too soon, whalers of many nations were journeying to the remotest parts of the globe in sailing ships, processing their catch on board instead of towing it to shore. Right whales—so called because they were slow, easy to kill, and floated when dead—were decimated, and later, the bowheads.

In 1857 Yankee whaler Charles Melville Scammon picked his way through the treacherous entrance of a lagoon in Baja California and found gray whales "in countless numbers about us." The grays, too, were annihilated, and in just a few decades it was no longer profitable to hunt them.

Steam outmoded sail, steel supplanted wood, and an exploding harpoon, fired from a deck gun, replaced the hand-thrown spears and bomb lances. An accumulator, which acted

The gray whale sometimes pokes its head out of the water. Old whalers called this spyhopping. For many years observers believed that the whale was looking around above the water, but photos revealed that its eyes were nearly always underwater. In this unusual photo the eyes are out of the water, although the whale probably cannot focus on anything.

like a shock absorber, eased the tremendous strain on harpoon lines. Hollow lances enabled whalers to inflate their victims so that even the heaviest rorquals would float. Huge, sophisticated factory ships increased the whaling fleet's range and capacity. The slaughter intensified.

Products that eliminated our dependency on whales, followed eventually by an enlightened attitude toward the conservation of our living resources, finally tipped the balance back. Grays, once close to extinction, have made a remarkable recovery and probably are as numerous now as they were before the days of commercial whaling.

Other whale species have not been so fortunate. Several rorquals, the humpback, and the sperm whale are still considered endangered. Some species, including the blue whale, may never recover.

Killer whales prowl all the seas. One particularly well-known group patrols the waters off Puget Sound. Scientists studying these pods of killers have discovered that they have a tightly defined social structure. Authorities still ponder why the animals leap out of the water, among other antics.

The narwhal lives in the Arctic. The male, and occasionally a female, has an elongated tusk twisted like the horn of a unicorn. In the male narwhal this tusk may be used for sparring with rivals. Like other Arctic species, the narwhal is hunted by the Eskimo. Even the tusk is utilized by these thrifty people.

GREG SILBER

The amiable beluga, also called the white whale, makes an attractive feature in oceanariums.

MARGO CONTE—ANIMALS ANIMALS

Porpoises have fared better. Too small to be of much commercial value, they were never seriously exploited by modern whalers. Many porpoises were swept up in fishing nets and drowned, however, only because they followed vast tuna and salmon schools. Improved techniques and modified nets, in addition to the diligence of National Marine Fisheries Service observers, have substantially cut the toll in the last few years.

Today the National Marine Fisheries Service, under the U.S. Department of Commerce, is responsible for managing most marine mammal stocks in American waters. The Marine Mammal Protection Act of 1972 established a moratorium on the taking of any marine mammal without a special permit issued by the Fisheries Service. Whales may be hunted for subsistence purposes only by the Eskimo. Some porpoises, seals, and sea lions are allowed to be caught incidentally by fishermen, but only under strict guidelines. A few cetaceans may be collected by scientists for research purposes or by oceanariums for public display. The Marine Mammal Protection Act has finally provided the federal government with the power it needed to protect cetaceans.

THE CATCHERS

After porpoises were captured for Marineland of the Pacific in 1954, the appeal of cetaceans to the public on the west coast was quickly recognized. Other species were soon captured.

The smaller cetaceans were usually snared in long-handled hoop nets as each animal surfaced to breathe just ahead of the bow of a catch boat. As the animal hit the strands, the net unraveled from the hoop like a sock. A 100- or 200-fathom line with a buoy on the end was then paid out to tire the struggling animal. Some porpoises were captured with a tail-grab, a padded, clawlike device that clamped shut on impact. Killer whales were pinched off with gill nets in the narrow channels of the Pacific Northwest. They proved to be surprisingly gentle in captivity. Having such creatures in areas where they can be closely studied has greatly increased our knowledge of cetaceans.

The bottlenosed dolphin has proved to be intelligent, quick to learn, and easy to get along with. Although we encourage such animals to do things for us, trainers have found that they are sometimes the ones being trained. This particular individual voluntarily flung itself out of the water at the old Marineland of the Pacific.

COURTESY OF MARINELAND OF THE PACIFIC

These false killer whales are perhaps exchanging greetings as they cross over a wire at Sea Life Park in Hawaii.

An imposing view of a leaping killer whale at Marine World/Africa/USA in Vallejo, California.

Watching whales has become an extremely popular pastime. From Baja California to Alaska, and also off Hawaii, thousands of people get a firsthand chance to see these behemoths. An enthusiastic group listens carefully to the sound of a gray whale spouting close by. We may be loving the animals to death, however, for too much attention may cause the whales to leave familiar haunts.

The Whalewatchers

Cetaceans may readily perceive the intentions of humans in boats. Anything that suggests a threat usually makes them wary. A gradual, gentle approach often does not alarm them, however. Sometimes they will even swim alongside a boat.

Such trusting behavior has allowed a multimillion-dollar business to blossom—and all that people do is watch whales. But some scientists feel even this could have adverse effects, particularly when the watchers press for too close a look and frighten the animals. In time, whales might begin to avoid areas where they have been continually pestered on previous occasions. Migrating gray whales may already be following new paths because of harassment, at least according to some authorities.

Suggested Reading

Orr, Robert. *Marine Mammals of California*. Berkeley: University of California Press, 1972.

Scammon, Charles M. *Marine Mammals of the Northwest Coast of North America*. Mineola, New York: Dover, 1968.

Wood, Forrest. *Marine Mammals and Man*. New York: Robert Luce and Company, 1973.

Although whales are usually gentle, a flip of a tail can easily crush a boat. Observers must be careful not to get too close because even an accidental hit from a whale can be lethal.

The humpback whales of Hawaii have become popular subjects for underwater photographers. Often the trick is having a lens wide enough to take in the entire whale.

Gray whale calves have proved to be surprisingly friendly in the lagoons of Baja California. Sometimes they will come up next to a skiff or raft for a scratch, actually allowing people to touch them. Here an observer from the American Cetacean Society pats a curious but wild gray whale. This nonprofit society is devoted to research, conservation, and education involving whales and other forms of marine life.

PETER J. BRYANT

Overleaf: A group of rough-toothed dolphins eyes the photographer with a backward glance. Photo by Gary Friedrichsen

Cetaceans and the Future

Simple economics often dictate a country's actions far more than any qualities we esteem in mankind. Had it not been for the burgeoning of the petroleum industry at a time when stocks of whales were dwindling, several species might have been hunted to extinction. Conservation efforts made by the International Whaling Commission on behalf of each species did not begin until hunting a particular type of whale was no longer profitable. It is encouraging that watching whales is now more lucrative than killing them.

Unfortunately, this outlook is not shared by Japanese and Russian interests that continue to hunt whales. They see cetaceans as a harvestable resource, another commodity to market. In Russia some of the meat is given to the Siberian Eskimo, but all too much of it is used for food on mink farms. The Japanese continue to eat whale meat obtained for "research" purposes, although political pressure from the United States, plus a growing trend toward boycotting Japanese goods, may turn the tide. A few Third World countries, together with "pirate" whalers, also hunt cetaceans, although opposition is steadily mounting toward them.

Certainly the greatest resources we have on this planet are the living ones, because they can replenish themselves, thus ensuring their own future. But whenever we take a hand in exploiting them, we should be responsible for preserving them. Our finest legacy could well be the salvation of the largest and one of the most intelligent creatures the world has ever known.

GARY JAMES

Have we seen the last of some of the great whales? Only time will tell.

Inside back cover: With faultless grace a bottlenosed dolphin swims away. Photo by Gary Friedrichsen

Back cover: Perhaps the future will see a better relationship between humans and whales. Photo by Flip Nicklin

Other books on related California/Pacific Coast themes:
Channel Islands, Death Valley, Sequoia–Kings Canyon, Yosemite: The Story Behind the Scenery, Big Sur, The Sonoran Desert.

Order from KC Publications · *Box 14883 · Las Vegas, NV 89114*

Printed by Dong-A Printing Co., Ltd., Seoul, Korea
Separations by Color Masters
Typography by Stanley Stillion